Walking

in

God's Shoes

Walking in God's Shoes

B. C. Bergman

B C Bergman

Publishing

All scripture quotations are taken from the King James Version of the Holy Bible.

Printed by DiggyPOD, Inc., in the United States of America.

First printing, 2023.

ISBN 978-1-7366394-1-2

Dedication

In memory of dad, who walked rugged mountains

and sandy shores sharing the Good News.

Contents

Foreword

"*Walking in God's Shoes*" will exhort you and challenge you to live the life of Christ in your daily walk.

Too often we profess what we do not possess – the patience and the trust that a true Christian should always have.

Daily, we face challenges and opportunities to be an overcomer; but we lack the discipline because we resort to living the "old life", with all its complaints and criticism, without taking the time to think that the Lord may have a plan for us that will be better than the plans we ourselves have made.

"*Walking in God's Shoes*" is one of those "Imitation of Jesus Christ" types of books, written in the language of today's world with today's problems.

It will help you, and it will challenge you to be a better disciple of Jesus Christ.

Gwen R. Shaw

President of End-Time Handmaidens and Servants

Introduction

When attempting to understand the actions of another, a reminder to 'walk a mile in their shoes' is encouraged. Although it is impossible to literally do so, a deeper level of insight may be achieved. Likewise, to better understand God, we need to strive to walk in His shoes.

Christians are commissioned to share the Gospel of Peace with the world (Mk. 16:15). Fulfilling this mission requires preparation. Preparation is the fabric of God's Shoes which provides confidence and peace along the way.

An integral element of preparation includes understanding God's Word. This is our guide or map. It illuminates the path and signals harmful dangers ahead. God's Word provides strength to prevent slipping when the terrain gets tough. When everything is shaking and others are falling we need to be steadfast so that we do not also fall. When the future is uncertain and peace is illusive, unwavering confidence dispels fear.

A troubled world needs a message of hope and deliverance. Jesus is *the* message of hope.

> "How beautiful upon the mountains are the feet of him that bringeth good tidings, that publisheth peace; that bringeth good tidings of good, that publisheth salvation; that saith unto Zion, Thy God reigneth!" (Is. 52:7).

The Road to the Cross

He walked the shores of Galilee
He died to set His chosen people free
He gave His all for them
Because He loved them
They turned their backs on Him
They did not recognize
That Jesus was their Messiah.

Jesus carried His own cross as He walked towards His crucifixion. The cross is the essential foundation of the Christian faith. It represents suffering and sacrifice. There innocent blood was shed to, once and for all, cover sin. Jesus walked the road to the cross in obedience to God's plan. The ultimate purpose of the cross was to reconcile man with God.

The walk to the cross was on a lonely road. It was an individual journey. Ultimately, sentenced to death, the crowd ridiculed and mocked Jesus. Even in the garden, before the walk to the cross, the disciples could not stay awake to pray with Him. Jesus faced the cross alone.

Some closest to Jesus abandoned Him in His darkest hour. Peter did not intend to deny knowing Jesus but, in a time of weakness, he did. In times of weakness, many do things they later regret. The road of life is scattered with mistakes and failure, but a step of failure should not signal an end to the journey.

The support of others can provide an undeniable benefit. Encouragement can boost confidence and generate a jolt of stamina to continue through tough times. We may take an extra stab at a task when we hear a confident "You can do it!" Marathon runners may get a rush of adrenalin as they enter that last turn and hear the cheering crowd. Fans contribute to the home field advantage!

Our race is not defined by earthly priorities, goals, or the fans. Heavenly priorities are based on God's priorities. Aligned with Heavenly priorities, Jesus travelled to the cross.

Doing God's Will was Jesus first priority. He dealt with rejection, humiliation, mocking, and outright hatred. Yet, He did not call out to the Father and question, "If you are with me, why are they against me?" The response of people did not influence Jesus. The response of God was His motivation.

I recall my younger sister's participation in a school sack race. When the whistle signified the start of the race, she carefully pulled the bag up and spent considerable time securing it at her waist. When she started running, the other kids had already finished. She finished anyhow. Oblivious to objectives of time, speed, or the first place ribbon, her motivation was the neatness and security of the bag. Pleased with her performance, her smile rivaled the winner.

Jesus was motivated by a heavenly purpose and was all in. He knew that His life would, ultimately, end at the cross as the sacrifice for mankind. But, He also knew that we were worth the price. Jesus went to the cross because He prioritized the will of God above anything earthly. Jesus valued the eternal soul. God's plan always produces eternal value.

When praying in the garden, Jesus experienced great anguish. The physical suffering would be intense. The stripes across His back, the spear in His side, and the nails in His feet are unimaginable. But the emotional suffering must have been even worse. The people for whom He endured the cross screamed for His death. He was rejected, humiliated, and degraded.

Why does America continue to help countries that dance in the streets when some misfortune impacts the USA? Why give compassion and caring when hate and destruction is returned? It would seem that those who benefit from generosity would demonstrate gratitude rather than resentment.

Jesus continued to reach out to those who rejected His efforts. Jesus taught the principle of loving our enemies. He lived using the principle and He died using the principle. The principle was more important than the way He was treated. God's plan was more important than suffering and degradation to the flesh.

> "For consider him that endured such contradiction of sinners against himself, least ye be wearied and faint in your minds." (He. 12:3).

Facing death willingly requires a conviction that serving God is the highest priority. Bad news, storms, wars, or pandemics lose their power of control. We can stand for God even when facing prison, a firing squad, or a fiery furnace. The Bible says that in the last days that Christians would be persecuted simply for believing in God (Mt. 24:9). Most of Jesus disciples died as martyrs. They were close to Jesus. To be close to Jesus we need to be prepared to die for the gospel.

Some start their journey with God believing life will be smooth and problem free. But Jesus said "In the world ye shall have tribulation: but ... I have overcome the world" (Jn. 16:33). Life is not floating on calm seas while sipping an iced latte. Often, it is more like shooting the rapids of a raging river with all of the bends, rocks, and fallen trees. Throw in a bear or two. The adversity might threaten survival but God supplies strength for the day and courage to face the storm.

Jesus slept in the boat when all of the disciples feared the raging storm (Mk. 4:35-41). Jesus had complete confidence in the God who controls the storm. The earthly mind will focus on the storm or any danger that threatens doom. It is easy to allow problems to consume our mind. But a mind that is full of God's promises leaves no room for fear and despair. Jesus knew that God held the boat in His hand and can handle a raging sea. God still controls the storm.

Jesus was not interrupted by bad news. The story about Lazarus (Jn. 11:1-44) tells us that Jesus did not immediately go to the dying man. He continued to do God's will. Jesus did not focus on sickness or death but on the God who controls life.

There is a cost to walking in God's plan. The cost can be unpleasant to the flesh but is essential to the spirit. Walking the road to the cross means ignoring the mocking crowd. Pain cannot be a compass for avoidance. Walking the road to the cross means following God's direction regardless of the cost.

Following God's direction requires obedience. Obedience demonstrates faith and willing commitment to God's plan even it involves something we would rather avoid. Some spend hours praying that a situation be changed with little effect. Prayer is a declaration of God's will over every situation not to tell Him our will.

Abraham was obedient to God's will. God's promise had been fulfilled in a miracle birth to an elderly mother and father, so why would God request this promised child as a sacrifice (Ge. 22)? Abraham demonstrated faith through obedience. He did not ask the 'why' questions. He followed God's plan even though the method may have been unclear.

A single piece of a puzzle may not reveal the picture. But as pieces are added, it begins to emerge. Each piece has a place.   When all the pieces are connected, the picture is clear.

Many search for purpose as they pursue life's illusive key to happiness.   Intuitively, there must be more than a repetitive existence.   "Got up, worked, ate, slept, but not tomorrow" is not a desirable epitaph.

Each individual is created for a unique purpose in God's master plan.   Some wait for a prophetic word or a loud audible voice from Heaven before mobilizing.   This can happen but, more often, abilities, talents, and strengths are a good indicator. Gods Will is not an unsolvable puzzle.   Why would He create us for a purpose and keep it hidden?   Our abilities and God's word provide guidance to fulfill our purpose.

Jesus knew His purpose and did not waiver from it. His death on the cross provided the perfect sacrifice for sin. All things were put under His feet (Ep. 1:22). Dominion over all principalities and power was achieved. In Jesus, the same power is ours. Even the lame can place the devils head under their feet. This is great news for any who feel weak. God is our strength. We are not exempt from suffering and persecution in this life but we face problems in the authority and power of God.

Suffering is associated with the cross. It is the price Jesus paid. In Christ, we have all of the benefits of the cross, but we do not pay the same price. If a friend gets severely hurt in an accident and part of the settlement is a new car, we can ride in that new car without experiencing the accident. Likewise, we reap the benefits of the cross without actually facing the cross.

Jesus defeated the power of death by facing the cross. Problems can be defeated by facing them directly. At times, this includes suffering in order to triumph, fighting a battle in order to win, and getting a few hits in order to be victorious. God is able to deliver in any situation. When God is directing our footsteps we can have complete confidence. We walk in His authority and nothing can stand in the way. He has our back.

Even in death, Jesus brought the thief dying on another cross to heaven. In the midst of problems, we can be a light drawing others to the truth. In the darkness, the smallest light draws attention. The darker the night, the brighter the light appears. Continue to shine and point the way to Jesus. He is the Truth for a deceived world lost in darkness.

Compassion is possible when the eternal end state of the wicked is considered. Darkness, torment, and weeping forever await the lost. Warnings should be extended to even our worst enemy.

> "For I was envious at the foolish, when I saw the prosperity of the wicked. Until I went into the sanctuary of God; then understood I their end." (Ps. 73:3, 17).

Walking in God's plan starts at the foot of the cross. The journey cannot begin through a side entrance or gate. God has outlined the way of salvation and any deviation, no matter how pleasant, will not end well. Every direction points the way somewhere. Will the lost soul find their way or remain lost?

Refining the cross to make the cruel execution and public humiliation more attractive diminishes the power of what Jesus did. Presenting Jesus as a prophet, a preacher, or a provider is more attractive than as a crucified sacrifice for sin. The Jews wanted Jesus as King not the cursed Jesus on a cross. Any alternative that diminishes or disguises the cross will fail to point the lost to God.

The cross is the narrow road that few find. Preferring a cheering crowd and the acceptance of friends, the road of compromise is chosen far too often. Worldly norms are valued rather than the separation God requires.

God will never abandon those who choose His path. As we turn that last leg of our race, all of heaven will cheer. That's when it counts for all eternity!

Study Guide: The Road to the Cross

A living sacrifice

Individual journey	Mt. 26:36-44, Lu. 14:26
Priorities/Values	Mt. 16:24-26, Ro. 12:1-2, Ph. 3:7-14, 1 Jn. 2:15-17
Obedience	Mt. 7:21, 2 Co. 10:5-6
Adversity/Suffering	Ro. 8:17-39, 2 Ti. 3:12

The Road To Emmaus

"If you are on the wrong road, progress means doing an about-turn and walking back to the right road; and in that case the man who turns back soonest is the most progressive man."[1]

C. S. Lewis

Many travel life's road searching for meaning and purpose. Reading the Bible, attending church, singing spiritual songs, and even praying now and then, without experiencing the reality of God is unfulfilling. Knowledge, without experience, merely provides a virtual reality. Many want to experience the real thing. The two people walking the road to

Emmaus (Lu. 24:13-35) experienced a *real* meeting that connected their hearts with their knowledge.

There is little information about these two people who walked the seven miles from Jerusalem to Emmaus. They were likely disciples or associated with the disciples because the text indicates that two of them (the group of disciples) left for Emmaus. Titles, job descriptions, or other distinguishing characteristics are not mentioned.

Everyone is on a journey somewhere. We journey to work, to school, and to other common places. Some know their exact destination and have a clear reason for heading there. Others may be escaping from something or someone. Some people do not know where they are going and are just trying to 'find themselves'. Others may be endless wanderers. It does not matter where we are or the reason for being there, Jesus wants to talk with us on the way.

It is unclear why the two people were on their way to Emmaus, but, as they journeyed, they discussed events that had transpired over the past three days. These events had climaxed with the death of Jesus on the cross. They hoped Jesus would be the deliverer of Israel. That seemed impossible now that He was dead. At least, that's how they saw it at the start of their journey.

Some reach the same conclusion when facing unexpected events. They believe for something and it does not happen according to expectations. Applying human understanding and logic, the two people concluded that a dead man could not deliver anyone. They did not realize that Jesus operates in a Heavenly realm that defies earthly restraints.

Jesus did not announce Himself. He simply engaged in the discussion. Notice Jesus response to the two people. He calls them fools and slow to believe (v. 25). He proceeds to point out that the prophets had foretold that Jesus would have to suffer and die to accomplish the ultimate result. He referenced scriptures that most Jews were taught from childhood. Many expected the Messiah but failed to recognize Him when He arrived.

Failure to recognize Jesus can be caused by religion itself. People can get distracted by rules and their interpretations of scripture rather than, simply, talking with Jesus. He wants to be real to us not a set of rules. Words on a page are dead, but when Jesus breathes life into the words, people can be transformed.

Religion is an empty virtual pursuit when reduced to a set of rules. Rules can condemn rather than aid. The Law simply identified sin and made it painfully evident that man could never measure up.   The death of Jesus provided a way of grace for man's sin. He was the perfect sacrifice, who died once, for all. Jesus fulfilled the requirements of the Law.

Even if the Law could be kept perfectly, does that imply a relationship with God? The rich young ruler had kept the law from childhood, yet, questioned Jesus, "What good thing shall I do, that I may have eternal life?" (Mt. 19:16). Jesus replied that he should sell all his possessions and give the money to the poor. The rich young ruler walked away sorrowful because he valued his possessions too highly to part with them and follow Jesus.

The heart pursues what it values. Earthy treasure is gold but in heaven, gold is just pavement. Heavenly treasure is the souls of man.

Jesus said that He would rise from the dead yet the two people did not conclude that he was alive. They knew that the women had been to the tomb and Jesus was not there. And it was the third day. The day Jesus said He would rise from the dead.

Even with evidence that Jesus can do the impossible, having received healing or seen others healed, yet, when diagnosed with a life threatening illness, some forget that Jesus received the stripes for all healings. Many have received economic blessings but, when faced with a home foreclosure, think they are doomed.

Jesus operated outside of earthly scientific knowledge. He was born of a virgin. He healed the blind person with mud and water. He turned water into wine. He expanded the loaves and fishes to feed thousands of people. He calmed the storm. He walked on water. He called dead people out of the grave. He defied death through His own resurrection.

Jesus said He will provide what we need — He will. He said He will heal all disease — He will. He said He loves us — He does. Any who do not believe what He said, are also fools and slow to believe.

But the story does not end there. At the end of their journey, they recognized Jesus. Their hearts burned within them as He talked to them on the way. Finally, when He broke bread, they recognized Him. They recognized Him with their heart. It was real and the effect was dramatic. It changed where they were going.

Jesus stills meets common people on their way to common places but a meeting with Jesus will produce uncommon results. When Jesus touches the heart it will have a life-changing effect and the road travelled will change, as well.

The road changes from the place where we hope something is true to the place where we know it is true. Hope is the initial stage but adding faith puts the substance in hope (He. 11:1). Faith provides the ability to continue in hope. Hope is expectation. Faith is confidence. Hope is the promise. Faith is the possession. Hope starts the journey. Faith completes it. These two people started the journey *hoping* Jesus would be the deliverer and finished *knowing* Jesus as the deliverer.

Rather than faith, some want proof. Faith touches the heart while proof appeals to the mind. Proving anything can be difficult. Historical events can be challenged by those who were not there and choose not to believe the event occurred. People debate the Holocaust even with a significant amount of historical evidence. But those who have experienced and been impacted by the event, know it happened. The real experience cannot be denied. Rhetoric, regardless of the eloquence, cannot sway them.

Logically, some acknowledge Jesus as a historical figure but struggle with accepting Him as Savior. A step of faith is required to have a relationship with Jesus. Ultimately, the heart must be involved. We must believe that He loves us.

Scientifically, can love be proved? Actions and spoken words may signal love but proof is nearly impossible.

It is interesting to observe two people in love. Awestruck, they gaze into each other's eyes, oblivious to faults, and blinded by passion. Across a crowded room, they can share a moment of intimacy. They have a heart connection defying reason and logic.

A relationship that does not involve the heart is different. Manipulation to meet individual needs is often evident. Commitment can be lacking making it is easy to move on to something better. There is an empty void when the heart is not involved.

Involvement of the heart introduces a level of vulnerability and risk. A person may have suffered a broken heart in a previous relationship. Protective defenses can produce shallow relationships. Jesus came to reach the heart that is cold and torn. Time may reduce pain, but, only Jesus can replace pain with joy.

The cross provided the initial meeting with Jesus but He is no longer on the cross. He wants to walk with us on our journey. He wants a heart connection. He wants us to *experience* the love of God. This changes the direction our feet are headed. Then, we become positioned for the next phase of the journey.

The next phase for the two people travelling on the road to Emmaus was in Jerusalem. Jesus ascended into heaven and then they returned to Jerusalem with joy as they waited for the Holy Spirit (v.49). The death and resurrection of Jesus and the outpouring of the Holy Spirit were separate events. When the Holy Spirit came, they *all* spoke in unknown tongues.

The purpose of the Holy Spirit is to instruct in truth and provide an anointing power. The anointing equips us to share the gospel with the world. The Holy Spirit is part of the salvation experience to convict of sin but the infilling of the Holy Spirit is different. The evidence is speaking in an unknown tongue. The anointing will work to break the chains of bondage and deception increasing our effectiveness in ministry.

The devil's kingdom is not threatened by dead religion. Even the devil can quote scripture. But when the anointing power of the Holy Spirit quickens the Word it reaches the lost and lifeless heart. The Holy Spirit points the way to Jesus and provides guidance to live in victory over sin.

A heart connection with Jesus and the outpouring of the Spirit can breathe life into a dead religious experience. A virtual knowledge of religion can be transformed into a powerful walk with God. Religion can be transformed from rules into a rewarding, fulfilling, and life-changing experience. More than empty words, this promise has been fulfilled and it makes a difference.

> "For the kingdom of God is not in word, but in power." (1 Co. 4:20).

When Ezekiel saw the dry bones in the valley he said only God knew if they could be revived (Eze. 37). Some dreams may be in that valley of death. Promises forgotten and hope lost in the valley of dry bones. Adopting earthly values and applying earthly logic, our passion for serving God, our first love, and our faith in God's word may have become dry and useless. But the dead things can be revived. The breath of God can restore those dry, abandoned dreams.

People still journey on their Emmaus road searching for life, truth, and deliverance. Jesus is not removed from common people on their common journey. He will meet us on our road and will try to reach our heart. Jesus cannot be real to us until our heart is involved. Then we can recognize Him as He talks with us on the way.

Study Guide: The Road to Emmaus

Meeting with Jesus

Reception	Jn. 1:12, Ac. 1:8
Change in Mind	Pr. 3:5-6, 14:12, Is. 55:8-9, Ro. 8:7, 1 Co. 1:18-28
Change in Heart	Ga. 3:10-14, Ep. 3:17-19, Col. 3:5-25
Change in Relationship	De. 6:5, Mt. 22:37
Change in Direction	2 Chr. 7:14, Is. 42:16, Ep. 5:8

Putting on Walking Shoes

One night long ago
In a stable so low
A little baby boy
Lay in a manger bed
And the star above
Marked the place where he lay
So, wise men could come
And worship the King.

Like the wise men of old
We kneel before you Lord
And offer you
Our heart and soul
These gifts we bring
Are like the gold and myrrh
For wise men today
Still worship the King.

Jesus started his earthly life as a baby. He grew into

a child that confounded the spiritual leaders of the

day. He grew in wisdom that comes directly from

God. He spoke what the Father told Him to speak and He did what the Father told Him to do. His pleasure was doing the will of His Father.

Every aspect of life begins as a baby. Talents and abilities must be developed. Knowledge and wisdom must be learned. The mind and spirit require a process of growth. A level of maturity is required before handing the car keys to our child. Likewise, the spirit must develop in the wisdom of God before spiritual keys can be handed to us.

When it is time for baby eagles to learn to fly, the mother will remove the soft lining from the nest. The sharp branches below make the nest very uncomfortable. When the mother returns to the nest, the baby will happily get on top of her wing.

Then the mother flies away with the baby. The first flying lesson consists of dropping the baby off her wing. Before the baby hits the ground, she swoops down and rescues it. Eagles probably don't care if anyone calls Eagle Protective Services. And they seem to prefer salmon over chicken feed.

The normal progression of our walk with God should be growth. The interesting dilemma is that the body can be mature while the spirit is still a baby.

Parents enjoy watching a child learn to talk, walk, and become independent. Offering help and encouragement, every accomplishment will be proudly announced to anyone who will listen. As my baby grew out of the drooling, teething, and diaper stage the relief was welcomed. Proud at every level of development, my tolerance for diapers was limited!

When babies want something, somebody better get it - now. Then, they learn to wait their turn. Then, they learn that important people get things first (or maybe they just make that up). Babies develop an awareness of other people, the ability to analyze consequences, and self-control. They start to share and compromise. They learn to play in someone else's sandbox.

Initially, babies are concerned about physical comfort and survival. They want immediate attention to their needs and on their terms. They cry when another child takes their toy. Then, they realize that another child will not share their toys, either.   And an adult may step in with some consequences for not sharing. In order to get along with others, babies may adjust their self-centered urges. Babies learn that they are not alone on the planet and life might be more pleasant if other babies are not screaming.

The struggle between self and everything else is continuous and constant.   Self evolves from complete selfishness to give and take.   The transformation from self to the Spirit is even more dramatic. Self must yield to God and then to the good of others.

As spiritual babies we depend on God and others to provide our needs. As we mature we become the source to meet the needs of others. "Surviving is about getting the blessing. Thriving is about becoming the blessing."[2] The movement from surviving to thriving is the maturity process. It can take time. Patience is essential along the way.

It is interesting to watch a small child wait. Five minutes can seem like an eternity. Tomorrow and yesterday seem interchangeable. Time can be confusing. 'Now' is the only concept of time that has much clarity. Maturity increases the ability to wait.

Our family used to travel long distances across the country. As kids, we frequently asked, "How many more miles?" My parents responded by singing,

"How many more miles" in an unusual country harmony. We asked less often to avoid the song.

When something fails to happen now, five minutes from now, or five years from now, does not mean it will not happen. The promise is not aligned with our timetable but is in God's perfect timing.

Some get impatient when the call of God is not realized immediately. Someone called to preach may wonder why a pulpit does not immediately open. Imagine allowing someone without proper medical credentials to perform a heart operation. The individual may have high potential but who would agree to the procedure?

"Study to show thyself approved unto God, a workman that needeth not to be ashamed, rightly dividing the word of truth." (2 Ti. 2:15)

At times, the training seems to have little to do with the actual calling. Pastors have started by cleaning the toilets or signing up for the army. Jesus was a carpenter. In these positions, characteristics like humility, faithfulness, and ability to come under authority can be developed. All are important factors in spiritual maturity.

Humility demands the death of pride. Pride opposes God because 'self' is exalted. Pride is Satan's throne. Pride is the open door the devil walks right through. Position and wealth are used as key attractors.

Pride was Satan's downfall and is the tool he uses to ensure ours. It started in the garden with the enticement to become "as gods" (Ge. 3:5). Satan will never recognize God's rightful place because that is the place he wants. He does not need to corrupt the entire word of God. A little 'leaven' will corrupt the entire message. Correctly interpreting the Word of God is critical (2 Ti. 2:15).

A key indicator of who is behind the message is who gets the honor. Also, the use of lies as the mode of operation never leads to a positive outcome. The means really does matter. Jesus taught us to pray by first acknowledging God as Father and honoring Him. The Devil appeals to natural abilities fostering pride.

Self-reliance produces self-righteousness, self-will, and self-works which place faith in the flesh. Faith in self is carnal. It prevents the Spirit of God from operating. It opposes faith in God. Abilities, talents, and intellect must be offered to God in the framework of humility.

Although, Jesus was the King, He demonstrated humility. When He washed the disciple's feet, (Jn. 13:4-16) His actions were those of a servant. The best we can offer to God is a life of service. As a servant of God, we will be ultimately honored. Each task, big or small, important or menial, should be afforded the same level of energy and perfection. Character reflects in the product. Give it your best.

Jesus came to do the will of His Father and to complete it (Jn. 4:34). Those who are faithful to complete assignments can be trusted. Critical jobs are given to people who honor commitments.

Faithfulness in small and unimportant things proves that we can be trusted with more important matters. Little things can make or break us.

Some contribute to the ministry through prayer, intercession, finances, words of encouragement, visiting the sick, or maybe providing a simple glass of water. Often overlooked and under-appreciated, they are scoring high points in God's book. The servants reward may not materialize on earth but in heaven there will be enormous dividends.

The servant's nature is to be under authority. Many have experienced the authority of a boss, the government, a pastor, or a teacher. Being under authority does not require that we relinquish values, beliefs, or ethics. Rather, we honor and respect those who are in authority.

I believe respect is given by choice. We honor parents because they are our parents not because they are good parents (Ep. 6:2). We give our best performance to our boss because they are the boss not because their leadership is perfect (1 Pe. 2:18). We submit to those in authority because they have been placed in authority not because they operate as models of our ideals (Ro. 13:1-2).

Submitting is not optional or based on an earned system. It may be especially challenging for those who are stronger, more intelligent, and more talented to submit to authority that seems less competent. It tests humility – but, isn't that the point? God entrusts authority to those who prove they will come under authority.

God places people in positions of authority. If He wants someone to give you marching orders, then march. Not only march, but march happily. Skills developed may be crucial in your position of authority.

Defiance to authority is a problem for any society. When everyone does what is right in their own eyes, chaos and lawlessness result. Laws require enforcement to be meaningful. If the enforcing authority is demeaned, the law becomes powerless. Definitions are distorted, technicalities are prevalent, and the powerful can purchase a get-out-of-jail-free card. Lawlessness is indicative of a society removed from God's authority. "Man has lost his sense of relationship and responsibility toward God and man. This makes him lawless".[3]

God's law is a restraint that prevents people from moving into moral depravity. A godless society leads to the erosion of ethics and morality. Instead everyone does what they define as right. A guiding compass and map are absent when truth is relative.

Lawlessness is a sign of the end-times. People will be "trucebreakers, false accusers, … despisers of those that are good, traitors, heady, high-minded, lovers of pleasures more than lovers of God;" (2 Ti. 3:1-5). Sounds like a fair assessment of the world today. Standing for traditional family, life of the unborn, and moral truth are, often, described as 'scary'.   People supporting these views can be labeled racists, bigots, or other derogatory terms.

Ultimately, there is a truth no matter how badly distorted. If a murder was committed, then there is a murderer who, ultimately, will come under God's authority. Then, respecting God will not be optional. He is THE authority.

Actions must align with God's authority first. Daniel continued to pray to God even though the Kings edict held the consequence of a fatal night with the Lions. God protected Daniel and He will protect us from edicts that are contrary to His authority. Blind obedience is not the objective.

Recognizing God's authority is important. We can align with God's authority or build resentment towards Him. Maturity produces a graceful response to correction rather than a rebellious spirit. Unlike the little boy, when asked to sit down. He sat, but was overheard, 'In my mind, I am still standing.'

Choosing to do what we want, how we want, and when we want is serving self. Importance and priorities are aligned with pleasing self rather than others or God. Just take a drive in crowded traffic. Traffic congestion is a repeat of the sandbox lesson. Can we just get along or do I have to get there first? Human nature prefers personal benefit.

The self nature yields to God as knowledge of God's nature increases. Awareness of the depth of God's

Love has a profound effect. The immeasurable, unfathomable, and indescribable love of God towards undeserving man is powerful.

It is impossible for the earthly mind to fully comprehend the love of God. Human restrictions and definitions often misinterpret God's unconditional love. Love that overlooks faults, imperfections, and failure does not provide a license to live on our terms. God's terms are still in effect.

God's love is not acceptance of carnal ways or approval of any lifestyle choice. Some equate love to a pat on the back and blind approval of personal desires. But God's love is the high expectation of a renewed mind and a transformed heart. We will think different. We will act different. Our desires will be different. Yielding the self nature to God, that transformation is possible.

Some view discipline as the opposite of love and resist the transformation. Resisting surrenders to selfish desires little by little. Justifying one thing, then another, can swing momentum, allowing the flesh to reign.

The self nature tends to justify, defend, and even ignore areas requiring correction. Blaming external factors and other's is preferable to dealing with personal behavior. We pray for changes in the world and others when God wants to change us.

Some think that removing obstacles like pain, war, and hunger might make it easier to do what is right.

But isn't that where Adam and Eve started? Every creature lived in harmony and their relationship with God was perfect. Still, they sought the single thing with a negative consequence. They were attracted to the forbidden like the proverbial moth to the flame. The fallen nature still desires earthly treasure, pleasure, and position.

Since natural tendency is self gratification, walking in the Spirit requires constant corrective action. This is similar to steering a car. The car cannot just be pointed in the right direction but requires constant guidance to stay on the road. God disciplines to keep us on course.

Those who love God will undergo an internal transformation. They value what God values rather than earthly treasure. Serving God is placed over serving self. God's best for others is desired. Service is a joy rather than a duty. Doing God's will is a priority not an imposition. Reading the Bible and prayer is a lifeline rather than a to-do-list.

When water is poured into a vessel it takes on the shape of the vessel. But when the spirit of God is poured into man, the transformation takes place in the vessel. The vessel begins to reflect the character of God. Makeovers in clothing, makeup, and hair have little effect on the inward character. When peace, joy, longsuffering, gentleness, goodness, faith, meekness, and temperance are on the inside, changes are visible in the outer person. God's love inside reflects on the outside.

Self improvement and rehabilitation are the world's method to transform man. Education, positive thinking, anger management, and 12 step programs are common tools. But God's transformation involves eliminating the old man (Ro. 6:6). Thoughts, actions, and desires become Christ-like and sin loses its power of attraction.

Arguments that stress progress and societal norms as rationale for allowing the world to influence and shape us are not found in the Bible. God does not fit into man's mold or conform to man's definitions. If God is to dwell in our house, our house needs to transform to His tabernacle.

We are an unusual piece of clay in God's hands. The human will can prevent the transformation to God's likeness. God accepts us as we are but yielding to the trimming, forming, and the fire releases our full potential. At times, we may feel stretched beyond endurance but tremendous growth will result.

Along the way, there may be times of prosperity or poverty. There may be periods of safety or times of danger. We may attain high or lowly positions. But through it all we can be content. Contentment is based on trusting God rather than reliance in possessions, positions, or circumstances. Contentment emerges from a position of faith.

Discontentment breeds complaints. Complaints are destructive and filled with fear and doubt. Disapproval is common and the 'thing' that will ensure happiness is always just beyond reach.

Many have been sidetracked by the Smiths next door, and their new boat. The children of Israel were there. They wandered in the desert and wondered why they ever left Egypt. They were fed miracle manna from heaven and wondered if that was all they would ever eat. They were delivered from the plagues in Egypt yet wondered if they would die in the wilderness.

Difficulties cause some to conclude that God's way does not work for them. Saying the road does not work before reaching the destination is premature. Heaven will be worth the journey.

The purpose of the wilderness was to humble, prove, and reveal the desires of the heart. That is still the purpose of wilderness experiences. Tests are to strengthen not destroy. The fire is to purify not annihilate. The goal is perfection.

In the desert, God will be our source. But we can also develop into a resource of God's love and goodness to those in need. Those filled with the spirit of God will produce an overflowing source of life to others.

In times of famine, God can still provide manna. In a raging sea, God can part the water, help us walk on top, or calm the wind. And, if that mountain won't move, God can help us climb.

Study Guide: Putting on Walking Shoes

Products of Growth

Patience	Ja. 1:4
Humility	Mi. 6:8, 1 Pe. 5:5-6
Servant	Mt. 20:26-27, Ro. 6:16-18, Tit. 2:9
Faithfulness	Mt. 25:23, Lu. 16:10-12, Ga. 6:7-9
Authority	2 Chr. 20:15, Ro. 13:1-2
Love God & Others	De. 6:5, Mt. 22:36-39, Ro. 8:28
Contentment	Ph. 4:11, He. 13:5

Walking Through The Fire

Struggling up the ladder
Fame and fortune just ahead
Reaching out for new tomorrows
I grasp to only touch the air.

The sound of joyful laughter
A distant memory from the past
Friends and family once held dear
Exchanged for nothing but the air.

Some trade fortune and fame for one moment of peace. Others give up peace and joy, to achieve wealth and fame. They reach for the dream and realize that attainment failed to satisfy.

Family tragedy, violence, abuse, financial challenges, career setbacks, medical problems, and a host of other difficulties complicate life's path. Fear and worry are common results. Fear can cause rational people to do irrational things. Fear becomes prison bars holding many captive to a dark existence.

Fear can cause a feeling of powerless without hope for the future. Confidence is shaken when the stock market is crashing. Walking in victory is challenging when crime is rampant on the streets. With an uncertain future, is unshakable faith possible?

The Titanic was thought to be unsinkable. Engineered with intelligence, built for strength, a technological masterpiece, it was the pride of the fleet. Who imagined it would end up on the bottom of the ocean on its maiden voyage? Vacationers boarded with confidence, laughed and partied on the journey; unaware that pleasure would be disrupted by panic and death. Trust in the unsinkable proved to be misplaced.

The first step in walking through trials is placing trust in God. Trust in God links to a force that is all-powerful, all knowing, and always victorious. Trust in God is unshakable. God has unlimited resources and is not bound by earthly constraints. When earthly logic and understanding yield to God's logic and knowledge, we can trust that things will work together for good (Ro. 8:28) even though some things are not good. The master plan may be obscure but should not be abandoned when we face difficulties along the way.

The negative scenarios that play unedited in the mind challenge our ability to trust in God. What if the mortgage can't be paid, food is scarce, the plane crashes, or an incurable flu is circulating? Perceiving the enemy as invincible allows imagination, fear, and confusion to bring defeat. Trust in God turns the "what if's" to "so what's". Regardless of the problem, God is with us.

> "For our light affliction, which is but for a moment, worketh for us a far more exceeding and eternal weight of glory;" (2 Co. 4:17).

David, facing Goliath, did not place his faith in Saul's armor and weapons of war (1 S. 17). He used his slingshot and 5 stones. Who thought that a shepherd boy, armed with a slingshot and stones could defeat the giant? The entire army had been unsuccessful. A tool wielded in faith, and an approach in the name of the Lord, changes natural outcomes to supernatural outcomes.

After defeating the giant, David cut off the head. Victory over giants does not come by negotiating, compromising, or co-inhabiting. Defeating giants comes through eliminating the source. Dealing with sin is essential or we will continue to fight loosing battles day after day.

Gideon faced the Midianite army, who numbered too many to count, with just three hundred men armed with trumpets, pitchers, and lamps (Jud. 6-7). Gideon's army did not even fight in the battle. They blew the trumpets, broke the pitchers, and the Midianites ran in terror. Those that did not run fought each other. They never saw it coming!

God positioned a small army against a large army to emphasize their inadequacy. Victory was impossible based on natural capabilities and strength. What we have is often insufficient but walking through trials is possible because God is with us. He does not fail. He makes the impossible possible.

Gideon did not view himself as a "mighty man of valour" (Jud. 6:12). As the youngest, from a poor family, he questioned that the people would even follow him. He felt inadequate.

God excels in transforming unlikely candidates into wrecking balls against the forces of evil. We may feel inadequate but our limitations are not God's. God appoints us and when we show up, so will He.

Ordinary people who felt inadequate for the task, but took action anyhow, have accomplished amazing things but amazing people, who did nothing, have accomplished nothing. When ordinary people choose to believe God and step out in obedience, they can have an extraordinary effect on the world.

God's plan does not imply a trouble free walk. Victory, the word, suggests a battle or struggle. God can give us a great promise and plan, but if the struggle and battle required to obtain it was known, we might not pursue the plan.

Joseph's life reflects the plan of God through significant hardship (Ge. 37-41). He was sold into slavery by his own brothers. They were resentful of his dreams which depicted his family bowing at his feet. What older brothers want to bow to their younger sibling? So, they got rid of him. But Joseph rose to a position of leadership in his slave masters home. This was not the final plan, through. Next, Pottipher's wife lied resulting in a prison sentence for him. Again, Joseph rose to a position of leadership in the prison. In prison, his interpretation of dreams for the butler and the baker resulted in a recommendation to Pharaoh that Joseph could interpret his dream. Then Pharaoh placed Joseph in command of all of Egypt. There was a great famine and God put Joseph in a position to deliver and sustain the country. In this leadership position, Joseph came in contact with his family. They did not recognize him but they did bow to him.

Joseph's path through life was filled with obstacles. Who expects a slave to become a leader? Who thinks a false accusation leading to prison is part of the plan? Who expects a prisoner to rise to a position of leadership? But, in spite of these setbacks, Joseph was positioned for the time of deliverance. Persecution, trials, and problems can position us for God's time of deliverance.

Joseph did not face negative circumstances because of sin or failure. He was being "tried" by the word of the Lord (Ps. 105:19). Through it all, Joseph did not complain or blame others. He proved he could be trusted in the ultimate position God had planned.

God will use people who have been tested, proven, and purified. He purifies by allowing fiery trials. He strengthens through adversity. When God is directing our path, trusting Him in every situation is critical. Adversity does not equate to failure. Trials do not indicate sin. Obstacles do not signify a path out of God's will.

A tough road is simply Gods training plan. God puts us through boot camp to prepare us for deployment. Those called to be placed in high positions of power will face more intense training.

The stories about David, Gideon, and Joseph point to God. It's not about our capabilities, position, or wisdom. Placing faith in God is the key. God's power defeats armies, destroys strong holds, brings down walls, provides provision in famine, calms storms, and renders pestilence powerless. God's plan leads to victory even when the path is unfamiliar. God knows each step. God still does the impossible when we walk in faith according to His plan. Faith results in action. Action aligns with God's direction rather than human logic.

Logic would conclude that the strength of a nation requires military might and strategy. God says that strength and prosperity requires a nation be humble and serve Him.

> "If my people, which are called by my name, shall humble themselves, and pray, and seek my face, and turn from their wicked ways; then will I hear from heaven, and will forgive their sin, and will heal their land." (2 Chr. 7:14)

God's judgment has fallen on a nation for serving other gods, rampant sin, and disobedience. Sodom and Gomorrah were destroyed when 10 righteous people could not be found (Ge. 18:32). When a nation rejects God, His judgment can result in repentance. Many call on God and pray when there is no other option.

To live in the covenant of peace and prosperity, a nation must recognize God as the true God and serve Him. Removing God places Satan in control. America was founded on Godly principles and has been blessed. Moving away from God by removing prayer from schools, "in God we trust" from our money, truth from our justice system, and the Ten Commandments from the public square, America will face God's judgment.

God's covenants are based on the path we choose. One leads to blessing, peace, and life. The other leads to cursing, war, and death. God's conditions are to love God and walk in His ways.

Walking with God requires complete trust in God. Trust in resources, abilities, and talents will fail. Man is powerless in an earthquake, tornado, hurricane, or other natural disasters. We are no match for cyber, germ, or economic warfare. Preparation, food and water storage, vaccination, and going "off-the-grid" are not enough against unknown forces. Trust and confidence placed in God, who is never surprised by any disaster, stands.

God pointed the sun, the greatest weapon, directly at earth. He placed a small protective layer around the earth preventing incineration. Yet, man thinks he is in control. Climate fanatics believe man can control global warming and rising tides. Louisiana, meet Katrina. Hawaii, say hello to Kilauea. And California, wait for it!

God ordains times of triumph and times of trouble. Peace and safety are possible even in war. Our feet can be steady when everything around is shaking. Victory can be achieved in spite of obstacles. Confidence that God controls every aspect of life must replace fear and doubt. God is with us.

> "When thou passest through the waters, I will be with thee; and through the rivers, they shall not overflow thee: when thou walkest through the fire, thou shalt not be burned; neither shall the flame kindle upon thee." (Is. 43:2).

Study Guide: Walking Through The Fire

Promises

God is with us	Ex. 14:14, Jos. 1:9, 2 Chr. 32:7-8, Lu. 1:37
Sickness	De. 7:15
Fear	2 Ti. 1:7
Finances	De. 28:1-13
Forsaken	Ps. 37:25
Eternal	2 Co. 4:8-9,17, Ja. 1:12
Refine/Purify	Is. 48:10, 1 Co. 3:13

Examples of Deliverance

David facing Goliath	1 S. 17
Gideon facing the Midianites	Jud. 6-7
Joseph in time of Famine	Ge. 37-41

A Highway called Holiness

"And an highway shall be there, and a way, and it shall be called The way of holiness; the unclean shall not pass over it; ... but the redeemed shall walk there: And the ransomed of the Lord shall return, and come to Zion with songs and everlasting joy upon their heads: they shall obtain joy and gladness, and sorrow and sighing shall flee away."   (Is. 35:8-10)

There is a highway called holiness traveled only by the redeemed. Pain and Sorrow will not be there. Tears will not be there. The sounds of war will not be heard. Songs of gladness and joy will be heard. This place is called Heaven.

Holiness and righteousness are essential on this journey.   Some   characterize   these   traits   as 'morality'. Unpopular in some circles, God's definition of morality is what counts.

Standing for righteousness and holiness can result in persecution even in a country founded on principles of religious freedom. Ridicule, physical harm, and legal prosecution can be consequences. Accusations of bigotry, racism, hate, insurrection, and even terrorism can be leveraged. While promoting acceptance and tolerance some are singularly judgmental to Christian views. What happened to *their* tolerance and open-mindedness? Someone summarized this point of view by saying, "There would be no wars if it were not for religion."

That statement contains a significant amount of truth. The gospel of peace makes devils and demons wage war. Engaging in God's work enrages evil forces that emerge and try to stop it.

God's people seem to be perpetually at odds with those who oppose God. This opposition is displayed in celebrations of sacred Holidays. Christmas celebrates Jesus birth but snowmen and santa take center stage. Easter celebrates Jesus resurrection but chocolate bunnies and colored eggs are promoted. Other religions seem shielded against corruption of sacred events.

Earth's problems were caused by sin which destroyed man's relationship with God. Earth's solutions can be found through restoring this relationship. Rather than acknowledge sin, many debate definitions, nit-pick semantics, and ridicule the messenger. Opposing correction, discipline, or accountability, 'science', without the required proof, is used to excuse behavior. In the end, God will apply His criteria and man's logic will be exposed as foolishness. It will be Gods way not mans.

The Ark of the Covenant, in the Old Testament, represented tangible evidence of God. It provided an indirect way for the people to be in God's presence. Only what is holy can enter directly into God's presence. God hates sin and the judgment for all sin is death (Ro. 6:23).

The Ark of the Covenant was built using the willing offerings of the people (Ex. 25:2). It contained a mercy seat where God met with the people. It is virtually impossible for people to be holy, so God's love met in mercy, with those deserving the penalty of death. God still offers mercy when punishment is deserved.

The Ark of the Covenant required precise care. It was to be carried on the shoulders using the "staves" or poles and was not to be touched directly. Carried by designated consecrated and sanctified priests, it was placed in the most Holy place inside the Holy of Holies. A veil was placed as barrier separating sinful man from the Ark.

Consequences of mishandling the ark were death and plagues. Uzza died because he touched the ark (1 Chr. 13:9-10). The Philistines captured the Ark during a battle and faced multiple plagues until they requested the Israelites to take it back. The

Philistines, initially, took the ark because they recognized it as a powerful tool. The Ark of the Covenant represented God's power. Using God as a source of power for personal benefit is an attempt to control Him. God is not in our control. God is not manipulated by anyone. His power follows His order. Walking in God's presence still requires sanctification and consecration.

Applying mans logic, rules, and wisdom in place of God's order does not end well. The Israelites thought they could test God. They threw tantrums about food and water. They turned to idol worship. They tried to manipulate God to provide for their desires. And man does the same today. If you are there, if you are real, if you love me, then you will do this or that. It is similar to the tactics of a child manipulating a parent. But God tests *us*.

God's power is not in the Ark, any artifact in the temple, the rainbow, any of God's creation including the angels, or any sacrament or ritual. Natural things are simply a way for our earthly minds to relate to God. God's power is found in God himself. God should be our focus.

Reducing God to natural terms fails to acknowledge Him as God. God is supernatural and the creator of all things. To out-create God, man defines the "meta-verse" replacing the universe God created. To improve on the human race, man imagines a "meta-human" merged with machines. Trans-humanism combines robotic technology with genetic engineering to produce 'a better version' of humans. Freedom of choice or the "will" is eliminated. A working class is created, who are really slaves designed to submit to the direction of the elites. The result dehumanizes God's creation. It elevates man to creator and diminishes God's deity.

Man's attempts to usurp God's rightful place have ended in failure. The tower of Babel is an example. The people set out to build a tower to reach heaven. One moment they spoke the same language and the next they spoke different languages. Afterwards, they were scattered all over the earth.

This does not detour man from thinking his wisdom is superior. Adam wanted to be 'as god' and man today is no different. Ultimately, this will result in the anti-christ attempting to eradicate allegiance to God and establish himself as god. This attempt will also fail.

God's presence is only with us when we respect His holiness and follow His ways. When the Israelites respected proper handling and care of the Ark they were aided. They were able to win battles, cross the Jordan on dry ground (Jos. 3:14-17), and bring the walls of Jericho down (Jos. 6).

The defeat of Jericho required marching around the city for seven days. As they marched, they were to carry the Ark of the Covenant. The presence of God was out front with the people following in silence. The focus was on God leading without distractions or words of unbelief. On the seventh day, they were to march around seven times, then, shout and blow trumpets. The wall around the city fell and it was defeated. Our eyes must be fixed in faith on God in order to defeat strongholds.

The Ark of the Covenant contained the Ten Commandments. They are God's requirements for holiness. Breaking any of the commandments is sin. The covenant, through the Ark of the Covenant, guaranteed God's presence and protection when they followed His commandments. The new covenant replaced the Ark of the Covenant with grace through the death and resurrection of Jesus. Instead of the 10 commandments inside the Ark of the Covenant, they are written inside the hearts of people. The heart replaces the housing of the Ark.

The heart is where God dwells and communicates His ways to us. The veil separating man from God has been replaced allowing direct access to God through Jesus (He. 10:16-22). We distinguish between right and wrong by God's tug at our heart and through His Word, the Bible. We choose to believe in Him and offer our willing hearts.

God, alone, is Holy, but we are commanded to be holy as well (1 Pe. 1:16). Our journey must advance towards holiness. This walk moves us from the "filthiness of the flesh and spirit" (2 Co. 7:1).

Filthiness of the flesh includes all sin. Worshiping idols, believing in false doctrine, hate, murder, adultery, fornication, and drunkenness are included. Sin is further described as transgressions of the law

(1 Jn. 3:4), all unrighteousness (1 Jn. 5:17), and everything that is not of faith (Ro. 14:23). Everyone has fallen into one category or another.

Filthiness of the spirit includes hypocrisy. Hypocrisy is failing to practice behavior that we promote. The Pharisees provide an example. They were the spiritual leaders of the church but they denied the power of God. They put on a religious outward show but, inside, their hearts were far from God. True holiness emulates God's holiness rather than legalism or man's definitions.

> "And be found in him, not having mine own righteousness, which is of the law, but that which is though the faith of Christ, the righteousness which is of God by faith:" (Ph. 3:9)

Holiness is not piety. The Pharisees put on long faces when fasting and prayed based on duty and form rather than a heart of love and compassion (Mt. 6, 23). Their words demonstrated religious knowledge rather than the heart of God. Religion was a duty not a joy. The Bible was used as a hammer on those who failed rather than to help them take corrective action.

The Bible should be applied for doctrine, reproof, correction, and edification (2 Ti. 3:16). It should draw towards truth rather than push people out of the door. It should point the way to Jesus who offers forgiveness.

Churches should be a place of refuge for those who need help. Instead, many leave the church after they have failed. Man's punishment can detour rather than draw through grace and forgiveness.

Man derived solutions do not offer life. Needles are provided to the drug addict rather than deliverance. Condoms and abortions are offered as solutions to sexual promiscuity rather than freedom from sin.

Those in trouble search for shelter, protection, and a place of comfort. They need care and guidance. Their heart needs a place where healing ointment flows. A place where tears are wiped by kind souls who know that, if not for grace, they might be in the same position. They need a place that points the way to mercy and forgiveness.

Jesus came for sinners. Churches should be there for sinners. Those who dress, act, or talk outside of 'church' norms need a refuge. Churches will look different over the next few years. They will be filled with people from all walks of life who are searching for truth. Teens that have tried everything but have found nothing. Rough, tough, street people with nowhere to turn. People that have never felt a parent's comforting arms or felt they mattered. Regardless of appearance or sins committed, we need to be the arms of love reaching out.

All have failed and need mercy and forgiveness. Some have sinned very little and may not be as grateful but, without forgiveness, *all* are in sad shape on judgment day.

Man's attempts at righteousness do not impress God. He defines righteousness and covers honest failure with grace and mercy. Failure is just a miss-step on the way to perfection. When doing our best we can fail and, yet, God forgives even at our very worst. Failure should never be allowed to destroy our faith or define our future.

"Every man at his best state is altogether vanity." (Ps. 39:5)

The walk towards perfection requires living righteously in God's eyes. It is a life committed to serving God. That means walking according to God's principles. Unable to do this through our efforts, God, in His mercy, provided the way of Salvation. Salvation is freely given though faith in Jesus.

Accepting the sacrifice that Jesus paid, allows us to join the redeemed that walk on the highway of holiness. When God looks at us, He sees us through the lens of Jesus who is righteous and holy. The cross is the narrow path few choose (Mt. 7:14).

The path of righteousness leads to peace, quietness, and safety. Ultimately, it leads directly to God. God who is "righteous in all his ways, and holy in all his works" (Ps. 145:17) requires righteousness and holiness of those who serve Him.

The Lord will save the righteous but His anger is directed to the unrighteous. So, why do evil acts of the unrighteous seem to disproportionally affect the righteous? Ultimately, God will have the final say.

The righteous and holy will be rewarded while the unrighteous will be punished.

God protects and guards the righteous. The Bible uses the symbolism of a breastplate (Ep. 6:14) and a girdle (Is. 11:5) to describe righteousness. A breastplate protects the chest area. It guards the heart. Righteousness protects our heart from evil desires. A girdle provides support or constraint. So, righteousness constrains us from evil actions.

Evil is the earthly nature (Ec. 9:3). The heart must be transformed to righteousness, the heavenly nature. The heart is changed through acceptance of Jesus, which leads to God. Then, as we understand God's nature and power we fear Him. This fear is comparable to a child who continues to obey the parent's rules even when the parent is out of sight. The choice can be based on a desire to please or to avoid consequences. God hates sin and there are consequences. The fear of God keeps us from sin (Is. 26:9) and the destructive path.

Constantly offering temptations, the Devil is sly in tactics to divert us to the crooked path. He offers natural or earthly resources. Horses are offered to the weak Israelites (Is. 36:8). They needed a defense. It appeared to be answer from God. But in exchange, the devil required disobedience to God. God had directed that horses and chariots *not* be imported from any foreign place. Different story same old tactic used with Adam and Eve. A solution requiring disobedience to God is not from God.

Discerning God's path from a detour requires a clear understanding of God's ways. The devil will offer a diverse selection and is equally elated when any of them are followed. Many religions, doctrines, and spirits (1 Jn. 4:1) represent the other way. But there are only two choices; God's way and the other way.

The Spirit of God cannot co-mingle with the spirits of darkness. Some involved in outreach programs to the homeless and hungry will be surprised when they are told that they are workers of iniquity (Mt. 7:21-23). God will not honor the right thing done in the wrong spirit.

The devil can quote scripture and make you *feel* something but sitting in his pews will be unprofitable. Looking for God in the Devils house will produce a feeling, a spirit, and an experience but it will not be God. The world's music, psychology, and education will not point the way to God.

When Elijah faced the 450 prophets of Baal, there were just two alters, two opinions, and two sides (1 K. 18). It was God verses Baal. It was God or idolatry. Baal represented all earthly religions, opinions, and power. The two sides were earthly or heavenly. They were asked to choose then and we are asked to choose now. Baal lost. God won!

Darwinism is another way. Attempting to reduce God's supernatural creation to natural terms, science is claimed as the basis for the theory of evolution. The fatal flaw in this theory is that the beginning, the very first organism, seems to have come from some cataclysmic event or big bang. Has a hurricane or tornado ever built anything but a pile of destruction? Science provides proof or evidence. Yet, has anyone ever seen anything evolving? Monkeys still produce monkeys! Every living thing produces after their kind just as God's creation is described in the beginning (Ge. 1:21-25).

God described His creation as "very good" (Ge. 1:31). Satan has attempted to "devour" (1 Pe. 5:8) God's creation since day one. But lies and deception will produce destruction. The other way is doomed.

The golden calf, worshiped by the Israelites, was another way. They intended to worship the calf today and sacrifice tomorrow. The other way appeals to the earthly nature because it is tangible.

The appeal of artifacts, rituals, ceremony, and sacraments is often preferable to salvation through faith in Jesus. But the other way ends in destruction and it is impossible to have it both ways.

When the earthly way is transformed to the heavenly, popular opinion and political correctness lose their power of influence. Friends cannot sway us to compromise. Leaders and laws cannot force unrighteous actions. Those who walk in righteousness and holiness follow God's ways.

The Red Sea moment when the waters parted, the Daniel moment when the hungry lions mouths were shut, and the fiery furnace moment when the 3 Hebrew's were thrown into the fire but were not torched are moments when the supernatural power of God collided with Natural laws. The virgin birth of Jesus and His resurrection, the foundation of Christian faith, is supernatural. The potential of the supernatural is foreign to the natural mind. But to deny the supernatural today is to deny the very existence of God.

God is the same now as He was then. He was supernatural then and is supernatural now. The time for miracles is not over. Get ready for a supernatural moment.

Study Guide: A Highway called Holiness

Defining Holiness/Righteousness

Sinless	1 Jn. 3:4-10
Godly	Ps. 145:17, Ro. 1:18, Ph. 3:9

Results of Holiness/Righteousness

Peaceful habitation	Is. 32:17-18
Receive Mercy	Ho. 10:12
Established Forever	Ps. 55:22, Pr. 10:30, 12:7
Oil of Gladness	Ps. 45:7
Exalts a Nation	Pr. 14:34

Walking in the River

Tomorrow is uncertain
And yesterday is gone
Yet, this single moment
Can mark eternity.

A moment seems so small
Weighed in the sands of time
Yet it shapes the future
So put Him in command.

On September 11, 2001, America faced a disastrous terrorist assault. Commercial airplanes were used as bombs to destroy the World Trade Center in New York and smash the Pentagon in Washington, D.C. The shock reverberated around the globe. Many felt deep empathy for the families and friends who were desperately searching for missing loved ones. The bravery and heroic actions of firefighters, police, and many others who risked their own safety, was witnessed. Volunteers came from across the country to assist. This historic team worked for one goal. It wasn't money, religion, politics, or self gratification. The objective was, simply, to rescue people who had been impacted by evil. The heart of the nation beat once more with caring and sacrifice.

Political leaders set aside the usual arguments. There was prayer in the Senate without the usual "separation of church and state" dissention. American flags were proudly displayed on cars and homes. The national anthem and shouts of "God Bless America" rang out. Out of the ashes of burning buildings, the phoenix of unity and patriotism emerged as Americans stood to defend Liberty.

After a time of grief and mourning, a path that determines the future is chosen. Some give up and the good things that remain are also lost. Others build a monument to remember the loss but then, embrace what remains and rebuild. Through suffering and failure, greatness is still possible.

Life can bring sadness and pain. Those who cannot see a way forward can become bitter, resentful, and depressed. But God trades "beauty for ashes, the oil of joy for mourning" (Is. 61:3). Even in times of tragedy, God's goodness can be trusted.

God thrives in difficult circumstances. A crisis, problem, or bad news can be leverage and re-directed right back to the source. Standing on promises and building monuments can reveal treasures buried in the ruble. They are often overlooked when things are smooth.

Churches need to unite and face our common enemy. The enemy is not each other. The enemy is "spiritual wickedness" (Ep. 6:12) and our fight is against the enemy of our soul.

God is coming for a unified church. Insignificant debates do not have a place in the heart of God. It is time to encourage brothers and sisters in Christ. Grace and mercy should be presented to fellow Christians and the unsaved world rather than each other's inadequacies. Collectively focusing on the devil as the enemy, instead of small groups of soldiers, the devil would have to face the united soldiers of God. Imagine the damage!

Solutions for high crime rates, disasters, and child abuse cannot be satisfied through religious theory alone. Quoting scriptures without the practical demonstration of the Gospel is lifeless. Jesus did not just say God could feed them - He provided food. He did not just say God could heal them – He laid hands on them and they were all healed. Jesus demonstrated the reality of the Word. Knowledge that initiates action provides solutions for a wounded world. Action aligned with God's principles is the objective.

Engaging in trivial battles sidetracks us and constrains the grace and mercy of God. Presenting the gospel of Christ in a compelling manner is restricted. The river flowing from the throne of God is pure. Self-centered desires and earthly ambitions do not contaminate this river. Water that flows from the throne of God is the lifeline that produces healing for the nations.

> "And he shewed me a pure river of water of life, clear as crystal, proceeding out of the throne of God and of the Lamb. In the midst of the street of it, and on either side of the river, was there the tree of life, which bare twelve manner of fruits, and yielded her fruit every month: and the leaves of the tree were for the healing of the nations." (Re. 22: 1-2).

The battle waged in the spiritual realm is unseen and often undetected. Circumstances are seen and the impact to the flesh is felt. Reactions based on physical senses are reactions of the flesh. Allies can be alienated by words that act as weapons of mass destruction. Reactions based on holiness, righteousness, faithfulness, mercy, truth, and love reveal reactions that flow from God's Spirit.

Thanksgiving and praise are key elements to walking in the spirit. In spite of grim circumstances, a willing offering of thanksgiving and praise, allows entry into God's presence where He reigns. Walking in the flesh, many remain outside of the gates of praise in the court of complaints. There, the focus is on personal welfare and God's failure. But, entering the gates of praise with thanksgiving, we find God who has supernatural power over any circumstance.

As the Israelite army went into battle, singers sang praises to God. This recognized the weakness of man and total dependence upon God. Praise and thanksgiving, as a frontline to the power of God, is indefensible by the powers of darkness. It shakes the gates of hell. It makes devils and demons scatter. It disrupts the enemy's communication lines. That is the power of true praise and worship. It might be a sacrifice. It might feel like sheep walking into slaughter. But God is still more powerful than any power in heaven and earth.

Sacrificial offerings of praise and thanksgiving prepare an environment for God. They produce seeds of faith. Negative thoughts produce seeds of doubt and fear towards a crisis that may never even materialize. Time and energy can be expended for nothing. A blessing may be lost in the process. Seed is sown through our reactions and will produce a harvest.

Pressure exposes what is inside. Heat will produce a bad odor from garbage no matter how disguised the package. The flesh will always decay and stink. The spirit that is fed from the river that flows from God's throne is pure and clean. The river of God is filled with love, joy, peace, longsuffering, goodness, mercy, gentleness, and faith. These fruits of the Spirit (Ga. 5:22-23) should be produced when pressure is applied.

Everyone produces something. Seeds sown to satisfy physical senses of the flesh produce a harvest of the flesh. The product identifies the seed that was planted.

Many can be unaware that they are walking in the flesh. A child may bring a bouquet of dandelions to a parent as a love offering. The parent accepts it with a big grin knowing it was given out of an innocent heart of love. But, after the child learns that a dandelion is a weed, the offering is no longer accepted with a smile. Similarly, God winks at some things when done in ignorance (Ac. 17:30), but, after we increase in understanding, He no longer smiles.

To produce fruit of the Spirit, the flesh must stop producing. We must yield to God's cultivation. The health and strength of a plant is based on cultivation and care. Similarly, without nourishment to produce strong roots our Spirit will be weak and frail.

As the Spirit is nurtured, desire to know God increases. Desire to know His will and operate in His plan intensifies. A compassion for lost souls is developed. Doing God's work becomes a priority. We long for Heaven and desire the presence of God. Living in the flesh we are quite comfortable in the world but the spirit desires to know God.

> "Thus saith the LORD, Let not the wise man glory in his wisdom, neither let the mighty man glory in his might, let not the rich man glory in his riches: But let him that glorieth glory in this, that he understandeth and knoweth me, that I am the Lord which exercise lovingkindness, judgment, and righteousness, in the earth: for in these things I delight, saith the Lord." (Je. 9:23-24)

Advancing past the pain or reward of the moment we can gain a perspective of eternity. Human nature thrives on self achievement, wealth accumulation, and recognition. Recognition from others is placed above "well done, thou good and faithful servant" (Mt. 25:21) from God. Our position before the throne of God will be in humility. All will recognize God's position. Recognition of God as exalted places everything else into perspective. It is simply amazing that He loves us.

We draw close to God as we adopt His ways. When speeding in a car, being near the enforcer of the speed limit is not desirable. Likewise, when living in sin, being near the enforcer of righteousness is not desirable. Allowing God to rule requires that sin stop ruling.

The sin-nature must transform to God's nature. Having a math background I am compelled to interject a diagram. For any who are math challenged, this will be painless. One large circle is labeled God's Nature and the other the Sin Nature. These circles do not overlap. Nothing in Gods Nature can be found in the Sin Nature and nothing in the Sin Nature can be found in Gods Nature. Unsaved people are entirely within the Sin Nature. Saved people are progressing towards God's Nature. People are at different levels.

The children of Israel were afraid to be close to God because of sin (Ex. 20:18-21). But, Moses entered the presence of God and visibly saw God's back. Afterward, Moses glowed with the presence of God. Moses spoke with God as a man speaks to his friend (Ex. 33:11). He argued with God. He was bold before God. But, he did not continue in sin.

God shines a light on the innermost heart and exposes areas that need to change. Self-centered ways are illuminated. A mirror, from a distance, may not reveal imperfections but, moving closer, flaws become painfully obvious. Walking close to God exposes character flaws and imperfections that require change or elimination.

The river of God is pure, clean, and clear. Water can be purified by constant pounding over rocks. When we feel pounded by life's problems, it may be the purification process at work. The purification process enhances God's reflection in us. Yielding is critical because resistance can break us.

To walk in the River of God, there is a cost. Selfish desires and earthly treasures must be traded for eternal values. Being willing to give up family, possessions, and positions is required to follow Jesus (Lu. 14:33). God becomes the priority and singular focus. But in the end, a lot of nothing is traded for everything.

The river of God flows from the throne of God. It originates from the position where God reigns. God defines right and wrong and judges violators. God rewards faithful servants. God is the control point.

God must be exclusively on the throne of our heart. Some sing songs exalting God as King, then jump on the throne for daily living pushing God right off. God is not interested in our song of praise on Sunday as we live our own way on Monday.

The walk in this river is against the current. Strength is required to maintain a firm footing based on Gods principles. Floating with popular opinion and society's norms can be easier. Political correctness and following the crowd is less eroding. It may be pleasant going along for the ride rather than facing the angry mob.

Strength increases as we stand against the strong current of worldly wisdom and self-gratification. Then God sends the rain as an out pouring of His spirit. Rain increases the water flow causing the river to move swiftly. This creates more treacherous rapids. Survival requires strength rather than fireside stories and up-rooted trees.

God's power in our lives increases as He rains down righteousness. Trust the goodness of God and be satisfied. Desire righteousness and be blessed. Drink of the Living water and be filled. Walk in His footsteps and be safe. In the end, all authority and power will be put under God's righteous reign. Pursue God and His likeness.

> "As for me, I will behold thy face in righteousness: I shall be satisfied, when I awake, with thy likeness." (Ps. 17:15)

Study Guide: Walking in the River

Characteristics of the River of God

Flows from God's throne	Re. 22:1
Pure	Ep. 5:26-27
Life-giving	Jn. 4:14
Provides Healing to Nations	Re. 22:2

Spiritual Development

Sowing	Ho. 8:7, Ho. 10:12, Ga. 6:7-9
Cultivation	Je. 17:8, Jn. 15:2
Growth	Mt. 3:10, Pe. 3:18

Walking with God

Who directs the lightening flash
And guides the tornadoes path?
Who holds each grain of sand
Against the ebb of ocean tides?

Who made the stars to glow
And hung them up in space?
Who controls volcanic flow
And makes a little lily grow?

All of creation stands
Ready at His command
The God that made the universe
Is master of my destiny.

A boy described God as " 'the sort of person who is always snooping around to see if anyone is enjoying himself and then trying to stop it'."[4] Sadly, he is not alone in that description. Those who hold this view do not desire a relationship with God. While God does judge the affairs of man, God also, displays mercy, forgiveness, and love. God's plan is to bless rather than punish. We choose the path that leads to the ultimate result.

> "I have set before you life and death, blessing and cursing: therefore choose life, that both thou and thy seed may live:" (De. 30:19).

Some question; "If there is a God, why do bad things happen?" Quick to blame God for disasters while slow to take responsibility for daily choices that result in judgment, mankind desires to define and manage God.

Throughout time, the search for life's meaning and purpose has been pursued. Answers to what happens after death have been debated. But those who seek to truly know God will find Him. The presence of God is similar to an overwhelming sense of love. "God is love" (1 Jn. 4:8). The heart forms a connection to the presence of God.

The Old Testament provides examples of the visible presence of God. The cloud guiding the Israelites by day and the fire by night represented the presence of God (Ex. 40:34-38). God talked to Moses from a burning bush that was not consumed by the fire (Ex. 3:2-6). Smoke was visible on multiple occasions when God talked with Moses and the children of Israel (Ex. 33:9-10). A visible sign was needed because they continually doubted their leaders and strayed from God commandments. The visible presence of God, dispelled doubt and the people were channeled once again towards God.

This pattern of unbelief continued to surface among the people of Israel. When the Egyptians came after them they thought they would be destroyed, they thought they would starve, and they thought they would die of thirst. God provided manna from heaven, water out of stones, and deliverance from the plagues that fell on Egypt, yet, when things got difficult, they complained and looked back at Egypt. Trust in God as provider, deliverer, and protector vanished. Doubting God, they wandered in the desert never reaching the promise.

The Israelites, who left Egypt, did not enter the Promised Land because they did not believe they could defeat the giants. God had performed so many miracles, why were the giants too difficult? Unbelief derails the blessing.

Caleb and Joshua were the exceptions that did enter the Promised Land. In faith, they believed they could take the land in spite of the giants. God's plan is that we reach the inheritance. Difficulties along the way can be faced with the assurance and confidence that God is with us. Walk in faith toward the promise.

When facing negative circumstances, we choose to believe that God will lead us to the promise or that the problem is too big. Actions align with faith. Action will either lead to the blessing or away from the blessing.

The Israelites often desired the things back in Egypt rather than the future that God had planned. But Moses turned from the Egyptian life-style and position to gain a Godly lifestyle and inheritance. He talked with God as a man talks with his friend (Ex. 33:11). The people were happy to let Moses talk to God and relay the message to them. They were afraid to face God's wrath and feared that He might consume them with fire. Those who walk in God's ways have no reason to fear. But, the Israelites were often sidetracked from God's ways.

God will deliver us from our Egypt, which is symbolic of oppression and slavery. We may feel hopeless and bound by the world's norms and views, but there is a deliverer who will lead us to freedom.

Faith, that God will help us overcome difficulties and obstacles, allows progress to the promise.

At the very moment of deliverance, we may face our greatest obstacle. The Israelites faced their Red Sea moment. Pharaoh let the people go, but then changed his mind and pursued them to bring them back. He cornered them at the Red Sea but God parted the waters and the children of Israel passed through on dry ground. Pharaoh's army was drowned as the waters returned. The children of Israel did not even fight. At the same time, God delivered the people of Israel and judged Pharaoh and the Egyptians for their cruelty in enslaving them. Those who oppress the people of God will face His judgment.

God decides the timing for judgment. He knows our heart and the true reasons for our choices. He is looking for hearts that are pure and righteous. Each individual must evaluate their own path. Individual actions result in judgment or blessing.

When God does judge, some question God's response. Just as gravity dictates that heavy objects will fall to the ground, God's nature governs His response to sin. He is Just, Righteous, and Holy. Sin is the absence of all of these attributes and deserves the penalty of death. This penalty can be delayed because God extends Mercy so often.

Though actions are often out of line with His commandments, God shows Mercy. Since "all have sinned" (Ro. 3:23), all deserve punishment. If Judgment was immediate, humans would be extinct.

It is more pleasant to focus on God's blessings and ignore pending judgment. Some focus on Gods attribute of Love and conclude that He would never punish. But the Justice of God will, eventually, result in judgment. Even earthly societies punish criminal activity, why would God not do the same?

The message is simple. The penalty for sin is death (Ro. 6:23). Universally, *everyone* who sins will receive this penalty. There is no discrimination based on ethnic background, religion, sex, age, culture, or any other distinction. When people worshiped other gods, walked in disobedience, and displayed unbelief, they received God's wrath and judgment (De. 28:15-68).

The other side of the message is, equally, as simple. The blessings of God fell on people who obeyed God, believed God, and followed God in all their ways (De. 28:1-13). Again, without discrimination. God will bless or punish based on His covenants. We choose our path but we cannot change what waits at the end.

> "O that there were such an heart in them, that they would fear me, and keep all my commandments always, that it might be well with them, and with their children forever!" (De. 5:29)

Many want the blessing but do not follow the path that leads there. The blessing is obtained on God's terms and conditions. Not only do we try to attain the promise on our terms, but we, at times, inaccurately define the promise. Earthly riches are sought rather than eternal. But, little profit is gained through earthly treasures if our soul is lost (Mt. 16:26). God wants to give earthly riches but seeking the Kingdom of God is a pre-requisite (Mt. 6:33).

Those who choose to follow God in all of their ways please Him. Enoch and Elijah are two examples that represent virtually faultless walks with God. They were so close to God that they have not, yet, faced death. What pleased God to extent that He would take them directly to heaven?

These men were consecrated to God. They walked with God. God's ways were their ways. They did not walk their own way and bring God along now and then. God was the heartbeat of their life.

Abraham also walked with God. Abraham "was called the Friend of God" (Ja. 2:23). Abraham had faith that what God said, God would do. This is a basic principle for God's blessing. Abraham sometimes wondered *how* God would do what He said but he took action anyhow. Abraham did not live his life according to earthly pleasures and treasures but he "looked for a city... whose builder and maker is God" (He. 11:10). He was a stranger to the world and the things of the world. His eye was on God's promise and he pursued it. People of faith please God.

Noah is another example of someone who "found grace in the eyes of the Lord" (Ge. 6:8). God was sorry that he had made man and was preparing to destroy the earth through a flood but spared Noah and his family. God looked at Noah and saw a man who walked righteously. Noah obeyed God's commandment to build an ark even though he was ridiculed. People had never seen an ark and it had never rained. To be saved from destruction, at times we must be prepared to look foolish. People who walk in obedience please God.

In the days of Noah, denial of God was prevalent. This led to a society without the restraints of morality and the guilt of sin. Corruption and violence filled the earth (Ge. 6). Moving away from God always moves towards depravity and evil.

Those who stand for God will be targets because they are beacons of righteousness. Strength is required to believe God while others mock. We must resist popular opinion, be labeled a fool, and endure persecution, yet stand firm.

> "Truth faileth; and he that departeth from evil maketh himself a prey: and the LORD saw it, and it displeased him that there was no judgment." (Is. 59:15)

David was 'a man after God's heart' (Ac. 13:22, Para.). The youngest son of Jesse (1 S. 16:11), a shepherd, and chosen to be King of Israel. He killed a loin and a bear. He fought Goliath, the Philistine giant, and killed him. A soldier and man of war, he won battles that looked impossible. He was a poet and singer. He invented many musical instruments. And the list goes on. But, he also sinned by committing adultery and murder. What was it about David that earned a place in God's heart? When he sinned he repented and he praised God rather than taking credit for his accomplishments. God was his 'strength and power: and made his way perfect' (2 S. 22:33, Para). He danced for joy when the Ark of the Covenant was returned to Israel because he could not live without the presence of God. People who praise and honor God in all their ways still touch the heart of God.

The children of Israel built a temple for God. God's presence, through the Ark of the Covenant, was in this temple. People went about their daily business and then came to the tabernacle to meet with God. In the New Testament, God does not dwell in external tabernacles. Instead, we are His living tabernacle and He chooses to dwell in us (1 Co. 3:16). He wants to be with us in every aspect of life. But He will only be with us when our business is also His business.

Like the Old Testament tabernacle, to be God's dwelling place requires sanctification and consecration. The world can see a difference in those who are consecrated. The world can hear a difference in those who are consecrated.

Priest's, serving in the tabernacle, wore special clothing to visually distinguish their consecration to

God. Their clothing had bells on the bottom so that the people could hear when they walked among them. There was visual and audible separation from the general population.

The priests entered the inner courts of the tabernacle. The inner court housed the Holy of Holies and the Ark of the Covenant. Entering the inner court required special sanctification. Each artifact required special handling and care. The penalty for mishandling any item was death. Most people were content staying in the outer court. But in the inner court, one finds the direct presence and power of God. Oh, that we might desire to enter the inner court. That we might be purified to enter God's presence and be called His friend.

Some want to be as close to the world as possible and *just* make it through the pearly gates. Are we "begging the devil for a place in the world, apologizing for our faith in God, trying to conform our religion to the mind of the world"?[5]

Serving God transforms us into His Nature. The process is different for each individual. "Work out your own salvation with fear and trembling" (Ph. 2:12). Pursue God rather than using justification and excuses to hold onto things of the world.

It can be difficult to hear God when we are unaccustomed to His voice. A friend, unintentionally, dialed my number when setting down their phone. I spoke loudly into my phone to get their attention but they decided it was mice and ran from the room.

Sometimes we do not recognize God's voice. But as we move closer to God, His voice rings loud and clear, distinct from the world's noise. Our Christian walk should progress into a friendship with God. As desire to please God increases, desire for the world's pleasure and treasure decreases. Living close to the world or close to God discloses our spiritual temperature.

God wants us to know Him, to draw from His strength, and to believe in His power of deliverance. Rather than a distant deity that demands allegiance, God is a constant companion. Rather than a temporary relationship when we need Him, God wants to be our friend. Those who choose to be God's friend can walk through life with one commandment: "love the LORD thy God with all thy heart … soul, and … mind" (Mt. 22:37). We desire His will, we honor Him with our accomplishments, our ways please Him, and our joy is in our salvation.

> "One thing have I desired of the LORD, that will I seek after; that I may dwell in the house of the LORD all the days of my life, to behold the beauty of the LORD, and to enquire in his temple." (Ps. 27:4).

Study Guide: Walking with God

Knowing God

Presence of God	Is. 43:2, Mt. 28:20
Nature of God	De. 32:4, Is. 55:8-9

God's relationship with Man

Blessing	De. 28:1-13, Pr. 10:22
Judgment	Ec. 12:14, Is. 13:11, Ro. 2:6-11
Mercy	Ps. 103:17, Lam. 3:22
Love	Je. 31:3, Ro. 8:37-39
Fear of God	De. 10:12, Ec. 12:13

Footnotes

1 C. S. Lewis Mere Christianity.   New York, NY: HarperCollins Publishers, Inc., 1980, p.28.

2 Samuel Rodriguez, Persevere with Power.   Bloomington, Minnesota: Chosen Books, a division of Baker Publishing Group, 2021, p.174.

3 John G. Lake His Life, His Sermons, His Boldness of Faith.   Fort Worth, Texas: Kenneth Copeland Publications, 1995, p.378.

4 C. S. Lewis Mere Christianity.   New York, NY: HarperCollins Publishers, Inc., 1980, p.69.

5 John G. Lake His Life, His Sermons, His Boldness of Faith.   Fort Worth, Texas: Kenneth Copeland Publications, 1995, p.443.